The Wound of Waves

AF410491

Refilwe Baloyi

Copyright © 2020 Refilwe Baloyi

All rights reserved.

ISBN: 9798667190400

DEDICATION

AS IT CAME UPON ME FIGURING OUT SOME SORT OF LITTLE
INDULGENCE AND SAID WHAT EXPLICITLY CAN I DO? I THEREFORE
DEDICATE THE BOOK TO GROWN-UPS AND ACKNOWLEDGE THAT
THEIR UNDERSTANDING IS MUTUAL. THE BOOK CONTAINED POETRY
RANGING FROM PAIN, CHEERING, AND EXCITEMENT. THIS POETRY
BOOK IS INCLUSIVE OF GOOD, MOTIVATIONAL AND BAD THOUGHTS.
THERE IS SOME SORT OF JOY IN THE DESIGN AND CREATION OF BOOK.
THIS IS WHAT YOU NEED WITH VARIETY OF POEMS.

CONTENTS

ACKNOWLEDGMENTS

Hello good people, your author Refilwe presents the poetry for the first time. You will profoundly enjoy reading the book. I would like to thank God for another opportunity to breathe and his Grace.   I would also like to thank my sister for using her laptop, and that inconvenienced her pace.   I would like to extend my sincere gratitude to my mother, grandmother, brother, and son for your patience, love, and respect concerning book completion. I would like to thank my cousin Daphne Dolo, and aunts (both) Tiny Mokwena and Johanna Dolo for believing in me. Lastly a friend Aaron Baloyi. This booklet is the result of your trust and dedicates this book to you.

Dear Son

Never say that I can't reach wondrous things, though thy worldly task full of trials.

The dreams, discoveries, awakening, and adventurous must all follow these things.

Though trials seemed false to qualify, fear not the unpleasant python

Care no more as fire flames fumes, though art the clothe lack

Never believe the obstacles of thy organogram cometh, no more fall of a great empire

As easy as waterfalls, that it could so unbelievable

Nor the lightning thunderstorm, consign to all your wishes

Say, I will return and all weakness will be unmuted

Fear not to insult, never say that it be a downfall

O never say I have nothing to live for, though art freeze storm falls

As from my timidities, nothing is impossible

I send this message, my son just to say I love you

Thirteen

You may forget what happened

But there are times she cries

She feels bitterness and twisted feelings

But still, she has nobody to confine

She never knew what to expect

Being called by the devout man

Still as young as thirteen tender age

But friend cautioned about a devout man

This was a man of God

Does her child sexiness provokes intimacy

Why are you tempted man of God?

Still thirteen

 The man visited her home for the first time

It came as surprise as a man asked her to sit next to him

She wore a mini penciled jean skirt

Being a naïve girl sat next to him

Still one of her shameful imbedded past

The man moved hands under the skirt

He moved finger inside

Into her gorgeous body, you gauge her pride

Touched her thighs

Still thirteen

Is she first thirteen you invaded her dignity

Still thirteen

Ugly darkling

Rejection is fate essence

Rejection discreetly alludes animosity

I am not yellow audacity

Then see ravishing confidence

I am brown-skinned duckling appearance

Still keep rise

I have brown eyes

I have an eccentric style

I love my extraordinary work as a woman

Shine on in and out

Unleashing soft spot

Lifting penciled dark brown eyebrows

An introvert in the making, but extrovert in crafts

My dancing steps inculcate self-esteem

I am not a choreographer

I love my short waved African hair

Music stimulus soul thoughts

Ugly duckling because of rejection

Phenomenal in the making

An inspirational shy ugly duckling

Church girl

It is half-past six Sunday morning

I've got to say Morning Prayer

Then brush teeth

Pick something to wear

I've got a dress to iron

My heels to wear

I'm so much in love with African waved hair

Ponder how to style my hair

On arrival at church

Hamming sweet melody

The pastor ascend stage prepares for sermon

The bible verse to retain

I've got to ascend the stage

Call to worship

Then half-past eight we sing the marching song as the choir (Siyakudumisa) on stage

Feeling like a highly devout woman

That's me for a sure church girl

Coronavirus

Now we are at a silent and no peace

Now we are the world of weary discontent

The population is enslaved of the disease

We keep longing for the vaccine

Scientist astonished and seek for valuable vaccine

The population moaning and groaning will tomorrow come

Experts astonished about the rapid spread

Researchers swept away by symptoms

Researchers renamed coronavirus as the acute respiratory syndrome

Is the 21 days quarantine curbing the coronavirus?

The population is feeling stressed when struck by fever, cough, myalgia, sore throat

The population is patient, locked down and many in need

A friend in need is the friend is indeed

The population do not lose hope

Advisers, Researchers, Scientist utters stay home

Now we will be at peace after locking down

Listen, stay home

Candlelight

It's difficult to put feelings into words

You always mean everything to me

Mouthwatering having natural rights and entitlement benefit

Worst fears are turned into magical blessings

I wish for our two hearts to bind for eternity

This love that cannot be expressed into words

Life without you is like dinner without candlelight

Brighten then morning stars and bring the hope of light

The best thing in life that's when you happened

Touched my heart and reached my palm

Let the candlelight joyful shouts be heard

Bless the day of birth and the day love created

Destiny lies within thy range

Use candlelight to conceal darkness

Candlelight is my frontiers

Worst fears are turned into magical blessings

Butterflies must never moan and groan of hunger

Why conceal each day the love is born with darkness

Gift of giving

When I was young, I used to see boys and girls with donation forms

As young boys and girls walked up and down

Gave up time for house chores

Gave up time for school work

Gift of giving the impression that no one lacks

With all your heart your shoulder is as the entire sky

In times of cry, you are smile

Gift of giving makes best friends like stars

As the winds blew in the sweetness

Watching behind the curtains the young rebels

Weatherly eager for school donations

Shoot for the cliff peak

Seizes the moment for a paid-up excursion for the crew

Content not to miss, but be among the stars

Gift of giving renders victory to the poor

Justice prevails thy gift

Greediness limit the world's ecology

When we come to think about it, **the** smell of perfume exhausts in vanity

And the aged values what is right at the right time

When the world ecological footprint griefs in despair, titanic seek thee sharing legends

All thoughts of a greedy person walk in with high heels, nature preservation dies

And children dress up in diverse flags of poverty

When religious gatherings send honor to sharing

And land mines utters for child labor, squalls falls on the head

No longer sense breeze of our unique and particular sons and daughter endeavors

And no longer lie in common goal for cultivating the soil

When the rich waving in the good, the poor trembles

All banners for sharing, limit the world's ecology

Up with sharing, up with the world's ecology

Fault

Nobody is born perfect

Nobody is saint

Nobody is entirely sincere

Nobody is better than others

Do not put the blindfold on

Nobody is pure and spotless

Do not judge other people for wrongdoing

Why are you thinking you don't fault?

Why do you hide your fault?

If you cannot see your fault, you think you have no-fault.

Faults questions your fate

The first dream solicit vision

When I come to reminisce about the first dream

And let my dreams steadily loose way, it solicits nightmares

And incense of burning vision lacks plans, and childhood dreams awake

Then I will confess that first dream reinforce the vision, with their eager shouts as eternal beauty

In collective shades of color, dreams solicit a castle

Do not hurry a dream, all dreams woes for perfection

Do not hurry a dream, but find a mission in pyramid opportunities

Nurture the first dream in the depth, flowing with favor

And vision stretches to the horizon

All power to fashion a dream without fear

A climate swings for a dream's helping hand

When I come to think of a first dream miraculously unfolds true prospects

Mistakes elicit discoveries

Yesterday I was afraid to make mistakes

Richly thinking, sensible I see right in them

And its ill-treat failures

From my end up in trouble, I make discoveries in them

Today I think it is right to make mistakes

Refining honest thoughts

Must our mistakes know our wins?

Bravery for the sensible mistakes

Yesterday I accepted my mistakes

Could a day bring brighter discoveries?

Life was all a harvest

Those who never make mistakes never make discoveries

Little you have

Little you have, the harder you work

The start of cheerful, pleasant creep

Tiptoe! Tiptoe! Thinking of magical charm

Tiptoe! Tiptoe! No good luck instore

Little you have, attempt to keep friends

Little you have, you lose friends

Tiptoe! Tiptoe! You can't beat the tense feeling

Tiptoe! Tiptoe! No floodgate open

At glance, reminisce at little things done

Little things you have, big things

Look back and forth realize little things actual big things

Little you have conquers the world

What to live for?

It is difficult to answer in words as to what you live for.

You will concern, you will caution

Did you ever think as to what to live for?

It is good to live in the world of fantasy

It is good to live in a little world of your own

Can I live in the imagery world?

It is good to say a little prayer about your dream world

Take time to ask a way to live for as is the greatest gift

If you want to be lucky work hard

If there is someone you can envision as hard worker, there's no else but you

If there is someone who can see light in what you do, there is no else but you

If there is someone whom you can count for your endeavors, there is no else but you

If there is someone who instills confidence in crafts, there is no else but you

If there is someone who talks sense in times of despair, there is no else but you

If you don't value your thoughts, skills, and work, no one else will

If you don't understand why you have to work, no one else will

If you don't know that nobody is perfect, you won't accept critics

The harder you work, the period changes

The way you work readily antedates passion

The harder you work, you notice you steadily reach goals in your pattern

The harder you work, the luckier you become

LOVE

Have you ever loved someone, who loves someone else?

Have you ever loved someone who reminds you time is not on your side?

Have you ever loved someone in the way you risked time and place?

Have you ever loved someone in a way you felt teardrops in your cheeks?

Have you ever loved someone so much in a way you kissed in the garden gate?

Have you ever loved someone it slipped your mind that you are a side chick

Have ever love someone you felt you could change his fiancé, be his soulmate?

Have you ever love someone who reminds you of the return to his fancy face?

Have you ever loved someone embraced his warmth

Have you loved someone who captured your little world?

Have ever loved someone you can't forget his name

Have you ever loved someone in his absence your focus shift

Anthem for abortion

When I consider how many lives are daily lost

Thy souls burnt to suffer

Labor denied thy souls

Rendered the talents useless

Buried the seeds, but do not have graves

Denied the world the opportunity to grieve

Doctors would say thy seed is a fetus

Who is there to hand out grievances?

Souls have vanished from sight

Souls murdered without a fight

Does Doth God need such an offense?

Mobs should whistle

Thy souls cannot be lost without a wrestle

Vegetation

Climate and soil necessitates his growth

Rainfall blossoms the defoliated leaves

Conspiring with him the upbringing of defoliated trees

Dark soil deliberately stimulate plant

With rainfall and warm temperatures

This gathers whistling tropical vegetation

Moderate summer rainfall, cool waters swallows grassland vegetation

Maturing sun, low rainfall silently mourns his death

Plants whispering concealed nature conservation prevail

Plead for Africa

Their nationality flogged them

They attempted to forge their identity

Xenophobia seized back to their roots

There was uproar

Their year was gloomy

The rulers, authorities, and people work together to restore peace, love, reconciliation among nations

The world contained diverse, race and tribes

Battle of Blood River is overpowered by triumph

Apartheid is overpowered by triumph

Immigrants astonished

Immigrants astonished

Immigrated to learn about the beautiful world

Others fled to find refuge, where is love?

World coughs, split and came to astride

Holy Spirit come down to the world

World glorify with applause

Young heart

I do not heartbroken

I'm walking like flying eagle

Still have days filled with love

Still young and restless in heart

Rich grey-white colored hair

Aging wrinkles make -up

Put makeup on for special occasions

Simply just saying I'm young at heart

Cherish every moment with a smile

Still loving holiday treat

Splendid memories

Smile

Conceal the innocent flower

Content with certainty that nobody knows

But deepest cut knows the innocent smile

Edges of time contaminate smile keeper

Content with certainty that smile intrigue

Smile stimulates mood

Smile get the day to the start

Calms chills

Do you remember your sincere cut?

Pause!

Relinquish sincere cut

Smile knows where you go

Smile knows your heartache

Home

The blessed child with sweet home

The shelter kept mornings and nights embedded squabbles

Best in millions

A day without a home is like a day in prison

In all the world there is just no other place like home

Best everlasting friends found in sweet home

When things seem to be tough

You are unforgettable

You are original

Also enclosed

Hugs, laughter, kisses, and empathy

Best everlasting friends found in sweet home

You are forever called home

In secret

My best friend sent up about

It matters not where you are

You always my best friend

There are times I wanted to kiss you

There were times we played hide and seek left home

It matters not

I am your best

There were times we had a favorite snack for lunchtime

You never disappointed me

You are special to me

There were tough times and stupid arguments

It matters not

I always counted on you

At night always grateful for such a caring person

It matters not

Because I love you

I wish you knew

I loved it so much

I love you

Lost love

Winter withered flowers, hurry away hurt deep inside

Your love sparkle, your love is like candlelight

Summer rains dry up, can you go back to the first time I saw you

Your smile makes me think of you

Each day, each hour, and the rest of my days

We shared laughs, autumn smells no defoliated leaves

Teardrops steadily send goodbyes, still deeply cares for you

Spring perceives no quality in soil

My love was once captured, I thought we were together for eternity

I have no one to love

Lost love

Abuse

Women and children live in a foreign land

Every hour, second and rest of days

Shh! don't close your eyes

Another human being soul surprised on ground

Infant soul's deprived dreams of opportunities

Stars become images of impossibilities

Ah, a baby is born into sour beginnings

A mother holds a baby in her arms, a bit of stardust falls to earth

OH, No! Sooner than you think you are alone

Ah, how good it feels? In a second I will be your shadow

Life phases could not reach times smile

Anti-clock wise antecedes the entire evening stars in the sky

The last breadth of every star fades in the palm of a man

Teardrops dry up

Foreign land makes no hugs, no smile, and no shoulder to lean on

Can you take bitterness and twisted feelings from man?

Can you instill heroic in a man?

Foreign land will be free if it becomes the home of bravery's there a way to change this?

Kalushi

Yesterday things seemed bad and going worse

Black, white, pink and brown drifted in color

Thy soldier's remembrance cannot be summoned

Thy soul sparkle in the new world

If nothing ever changed there would be no heroes

Can I refill the sea teardrops?

Nation sighed, woes and moans thy vanished soul

For thy precious friend lay to rest in youth tame

Thy hero traveled around African neighboring to make a difference

Then I think of thee special friend

There is no distance between thy spirit and thee a land

Thy forgone soul soldier and remembrance of hero

Thy rebel with thee deepest cut

Restless nights of grievances gift

Giggles, cry, blood split and sentencing

Watching behind the prison walls

Voices of ancestral spirits

Footprints up and down

Forfeited all life's beautiful seasons

Thy hero took court journey confronted guerilla tactic

The Bright morning light the fourth generations

Now thy soul lay to sleep

Thy soul song in the freedom

Humanity thy soldier's greatest attribute

Thy spirit gave life and love for freedom

Let the world be grateful for people who gave victory

Lala Land

And I will comment upon la land

Speak of my love, and I will sigh

Over the cliff, over the mountain

Through the valley, through the sea

I do wonder if anywhere that there is someone like you

And I adore thee twinkling star

Always shines like gold

Wished to dance at least two steps for thee

Those are candies, those be butterflies

The new Lala adventurous land

Shoot for the moon in the centuries

Seek thy earnest purity

And happily of thy sweet love melody

Dear Sister

Because though art not seen, each moment lived in

Most friendship merely perish, his life full of thy bitter paradise

But in their tone, thy dream shattered in

Though thou faint heart bite so imminent paradise

Rose's smells eloquent, not everyone rose as honest as smell perceives

With her innocence, licking her heels fit seizes

As benefits sting, although thy rose smells rude

Unfriendly the smells ingratitude's

As seasons blow by blow, shoot, shoot to the friendly sky

Fear no more the prominent smell, as the suns light brightens on

Nor thee bitter paradise rages, as the friendly sky smiles

Though hast finished smells breadth, still keep rise on

Alone

Must all follow this? In sweet music fine art souls

In dancing moves overarching sea waves, then sing to mysteries

And foresee the climb of mountain freeze, shout out to springs

Abandoning the grief of heart, caring for slumber nights of sleep

Matte pillows before sleep, sing slumber good sleeps

Refine the peaceful sleep, falls nights of sleep

Play in the morning, the toddler's past games

Lifting head, watching through window sun radiates

Even the pillows pillar strength in deep sleep

Anxieties bow themselves, then begin to sings

Everything that hit stroke killing self-love, matte the deep rests

As water showers, loneliness fades

Be still

Nourish griefs with intriguing dimples, cry no more

Let sighs fades, eradicate dumps

No more sing with a scratchy voice, cry no more

And be ever so much kind to thyself, O much more embrace inner beauty

By that natural sweet odor dims despairs

And unmasked natural beauty looks fair, so vibrant indeed

But, for the virtue of treasure star vested in thee be still

Blossoms from fair-minded, that fond desire

Be still bestows fond memory, past creep making feminine goddess

That from fairest lively red rose, content with riper aptitude

Thyself deems still waters fresh, contented within thy own scarlet eyes

ABOUT THE AUTHOR

Refilwe Baloyi is a poet and novelist. Today she's the first time poetry book writer would like to write more books. Refilwe has the B: Commerce in Financial Management attained at the University of South Africa. Refilwe believer of being a lifelong writer. In the writer's journey Refilwe wishes to be a fiction and non-fiction writer.

www.ingramcontent.com/pod-product-compliance
Lightning Source LLC
Chambersburg PA
CBHW061410160726
47995CB00002B/548